# "GONE WITH THE WIND"™

# COOK BOOK

# "GONE WITH THE WIND"™

# COOK BOOK

### Facsimile Edition

### Inspired by the picture
### "GONE WITH THE WIND"

**A Selznick International Picture**

PRODUCED BY DAVID O. SELZNICK

A Metro · Goldwyn · Mayer Release

## Abbeville Press, Inc.
## New York · London · Paris

# TABLE OF CONTENTS

# FOREWORD

❧ "GONE WITH THE WIND" *told of a style of living, as well as a romantic drama. A way of living and playing and eating that thrilled us all.*

❧ *Undoubtedly many of you, after you enjoyed the recent photoplay* GONE WITH THE WIND, *carried away mental pictures of the pretty ladies blushing daintily behind their fans; of the men riding, hunting and fishing, or with noses buried deep in mint leaves. Perhaps, too, you may have seen, in your mind's eye, that polished mahogany dining table at Tara, reflecting a juicy baked ham at one end, a veritable mountain of fried chicken at the other, and crowding in between corn muffins, hot biscuits, and waffles oozing with butter; heaping dishes of fried squash, stewed okra, and collards swimming in rich liquor; pecan pie, rich, steaming plum pudding, pound cake topped with sweetened whipped cream, and fluffy, white Syllabub fragrant of the wine cellar. Though many of these pictures in reality died before your very eyes, still the memory of them carries on.*

❧ *Yes, it is all a picture of southern hospitality and southern food of that era. And a picture we do not like to lose.*

❧ *Hence we collected the southern recipes for this book*  *ing you would like to keep their deliciousness alive by serving them at dinner, luncheon or bridge parties. Surely the members of your family will enjoy the Lacy Corn Cakes, Scarlett's thick Crab and Okra Gumbo, Aunt Pittypat's delicate Cocoanut Pudding, or Melanie's Sweet Potato Pie.*

❧ *We hope you will enjoy reading, making and serving these southern recipes in your home.*

# ⟨ SUGGESTIONS ⟩

## *for* "GONE WITH THE WIND" *Parties*

*Note of advice to young girls: If you are so fortunate as to receive an invitation to any of these parties, better not yield to Mammy's admonitions and go fortified with a trayful of buckwheat cakes with syrup, a large slice of ham, and baked yams with butter. Ladies may eat heartily in public today and still be ladies—for we have learned to depend on athletics, and not on tight lacing to keep a seventeen-inch waist line!*

### DINNER PARTY

Southern Vegetable Soup (p.6)
Tidewater Country Fried
Soft-shelled Crabs (p.15)
Southern Fried Chicken (p.12)
Gerald O'Hara Ham Steak (p.9)
Boiled Okra or Squash (p.28)
Candied Yams (p.28)
Buttermilk Biscuits (p.21)
and Creamed Scones (p.24)
Green Salad Bowl (p.30)
with Roquefort Dressing (p.29)
Aunt Pittypat's Coconut
Pudding (p.39) or Plantation
Pumpkin Pie (p.43)
Coffee     Pralines

### LUNCHEON PARTY

Broiled Oysters
on the Half Shell (p.15)
Chicken Pilau (p.17)
Vegetable Salad Bowl (p.17)
Baking Powder Biscuits (p.29)
Sally Lunn (p.26)
Egg Nog Ice Cream (p.24)
or Frozen Syllabub (p.42)
Lady Baltimore Cake (p.44)
Coffee (p.34)

### SUNDAY NIGHT SUPPER

Brunswick Stew (p.12)
Celery     Olives     Pickles
Green Salad Bowl (p.30)
French Dressing (p.29)
Cracklin Bread (p.24)
Watermelon Slices
or Ambrosia (p.44)

# ᴄᴏ SOUPS ᴄᴏ

**ALL** FAMILIAR SOUPS *from the Southland are indicative of the foods produced there: oysters and other seafoods from the shore countries, rice from its lowlands, and okra, turnips, and members of the pork family are used without stint. Outstanding among them are the New Orleans Gumbos. These rich soups are French in origin and seasoned by the Indian ingredient filé powder (ground and dried sassafras leaves).*

## ⟶ LOUISIANA CHICKEN GUMBO ⟵

| | |
|---|---|
| 1 small (3-pound) fowl | 2 cups sliced okra |
| 4 tablespoons fat, butter or bacon fat | 1 sprig thyme |
| 1 slice (1-pound) ham, diced | 2 dozen oysters |
| 1 medium onion, sliced | 1/16 teaspoon cayenne |
| 1½ teaspoons salt | 1 tablespoon filé or |
| 1 quart hot water | 3 tablespoons ... leaves |

Cooked rice

Clean chicken and cut in pieces. Sauté chicken in fat in heavy frying pan until browned, turning frequently. Add ham and onion, and sauté about 10 minutes. Add salt and water; bring to a boil, and simmer about 1½ hours, or until chicken is tender. Add okra and thyme, and simmer ½ hour longer, or until okra is tender. Remove chicken from bone and return to stock. Add oysters and cayenne, and cook until edges of oysters curl. Add additional seasoning if needed. Just before serving stir in filé or sassafras leaves. Serve at once in hot tureen with boiled rice, or serve in hot soup bowls. Makes 6 to 8 servings.

## ➤ SOUTHERN OYSTER SOUP ➤

| | |
|---|---|
| 1 cup oyster liquor | ½ teaspoon mace |
| 2 dozen oysters | ⅛ teaspoon salt |
| 6 cups milk | Dash of pepper |
| 4 tablespoons butter | Paprika |

Heat oyster liquor to boiling point. Add oysters and simmer until edges curl. Scald milk; add butter, oysters, liquor, and seasonings. Serve at once in hot soup bowls with a dash of paprika over soup. Makes 6 servings.

## ➤ SOUTHLAND VEGETABLE SOUP ➤

| | |
|---|---|
| 1 small soup bone (knuckle) | ⅓ cup chopped onion |
| Cold water to cover | ¾ cup chopped celery leaves and stalks |
| ½ cup diced white turnip | 2½ cups (No. 2 can) tomatoes |
| 1½ cups diced carrots | 2 teaspoons salt |
| 1 cup diced potatoes | ⅛ teaspoon pepper |

Wipe meat with a damp cloth. Place in kettle, add water to cover, heat slowly to boiling point, and boil 10 minutes. Cover and simmer 3 hours, removing scum as it forms. Add vegetables and seasonings, and continue simmering for another hour. Remove soup bone and pour soup into hot tureen or bowls. Makes 6 servings.

## ➤ CRAB AND OKRA GUMBO ➤

| | |
|---|---|
| 4 hard-shell crabs | 4 green onions |
| 1 pound shrimp, cooked | 1 small clove garlic, chopped fine |
| ½ pound raw ham | 1½ quarts boiling water |
| 2 tablespoons salad oil | 1 pound okra, cut small |
| 2 tablespoons flour | Salt and pepper to taste |
| 3 slices bacon | Cooked rice |
| 1 can tomato paste or 1 small can tomatoes | |

Clean the crabs, remove all meat from claws and body, and cut into pieces; each crab will make 4 to 6 pieces. Shell the shrimp. Cut ham and bacon into small pieces. Mix the flour and oil in a pot. When brown add bacon and ham. Cook for a few minutes, and add crab and shrimp. Let this mixture cook until it becomes a good brown. Add onion and garlic to crab and shrimp. Pour in water slowly, then add okra, seasonings and tomato paste. Cook slowly, stirring frequently, about 1 hour, or until it begins to thicken. A lid should be kept on the pot. Serve hot with dry, cooked rice. If it gets too thick, more water can be added. Serves 6 to 8.

# ✧ MEATS ✧

PERHAPS MANY OF US *can never actually experience but we can imagine the real Georgia barbecue—fresh pork and mutton by the pit-full, roasted over hickory log coals, and spiced with the sharp barbecue sauce. What picnics they must have had at Tara! But you can make Barbecued Spareribs at home. You need never be without juicy baked glazed hams, platters of fried chicken, rich kidney stew on your tables.*

## ➤ TARA PORK, SCRAMBLE ➤

| | |
|---|---|
| 4 slices salt pork | 1 (12-ounce) can whole kernel corn |
| 6 eggs, slightly beaten | 1 cup milk |
| Dash of pepper | |

Dice salt pork and fry until brown; pour off all but 3 tablespoons of the fat. Add mixture of egg, corn, milk, and pepper to pork fryings. Add salt if needed. Cook over low heat, stirring constantly until set. Makes 6 servings.

## ➤ CHICKEN-FRIED STEAK ➤

| | |
|---|---|
| 2 pounds round steak, ¾-inch thick | Flour |
| Salt and pepper | 4 tablespoons chopped suet, water |

Rub steak liberally with salt and pepper; pound as much flour into it as possible. Brown slowly on both sides in hot cooking fat. Add a tablespoon or two of water; cover, and steam or simmer a few minutes to make fork-tender. Makes 6 servings.

As far back as can be remembered, "chicken-fried steak" has been a favorite main dish in the South. The simple process of its preparation, and its ultimate tastiness, makes it an old favorite.

## ➤ JELLY GLAZING FOR TURKEY OR HAM ➤

Roast turkey or ham, hot                          ½ to 1 cup tart jelly (grape or currant)
          ⅛ to ½ cup stock or drippings in pan

Beat jelly with fork or egg beater to break it up; add hot stock
and brush over hot turkey or ham during the last half hour of
roasting, basting several times with mixture, and using drippings
in pan.

For roast leg of lamb, add ¼ cup chopped mint to jelly and use
lamb drippings in pan instead of turkey stock. Proceed as for
turkey.

## ➤ VEAL AND RICE CASSEROLE ➤

| | |
|---|---|
| 4 small slices salt pork, diced | 1 cup steamed rice |
| 1 large onion, chopped | 1 can tomato paste OR |
| 4 cups cooked diced veal | 1 can tomato soup |
| Salt and pepper | 2 hard-cooked eggs |
| 1 cup water | 2 tablespoons butter or margarine |

Fry salt pork and onion about 10 minutes or until lightly
browned. Add veal, seasonings as needed, and water; heat through.
Pour into well-greased baking dish; cover with mixture of rice
and tomato paste; slice eggs on top. Dot with butter or margarine.
Cover, and bake in moderate oven (350 degrees F.) 30 minutes, adding a little water from time to time if necessary. Makes 4 to 6
servings.

## ➤ LAMB AND RICE CASSEROLE ➤

Make above recipe using 3 tablespoons salad oil in place of salt
pork, use cooked chopped lamb for veal; add ⅛ teaspoon thyme for
seasoning.

## ➤ BAKED STUFFED PORK CHOPS ➤

| | |
|---|---|
| 6 thick rib pork chops | Salt and pepper |
| Bread stuffing | 1 cup fine bread crumbs |
| 1 egg, lightly beaten | ¼ cup fat |
| 2 tablespoons water | ½ cup hot water |

Have chops cut about 2 inches thick, with pocket for dressing in
each. Fill with a savory stuffing and fasten with small skewers.
Dip chops in egg mixed with water; sprinkle with salt and pepper,
and dredge with crumbs. Brown both sides in fat; add hot water.
Cover, and bake in moderate oven (350 degrees F.) for 1 hour or
until tender. Makes 6 servings.

# ➤➤ BARBECUED SPARERIBS ➤

| | |
|---|---|
| 4 pounds spareribs | ¾ cup water |
| 2 medium-sized onions, sliced | 2 tablespoons vinegar |
| 2 teaspoons salt | 2 teaspoons Worcestershire sauce |
| ¼ teaspoon pepper | ⅛ teaspoon cayenne |
| ¾ cup catsup | 1 teaspoon chili powder |

Arrange spareribs in large baking dish or roaster. Add onions, and sprinkle with salt and pepper. Combine remaining ingredients, and pour over spareribs. Cover, and bake in moderate oven (350 degrees F.) about 1½ hours, basting frequently. Remove cover, and bake 20 minutes longer. Makes 6 servings.

# ➤➤ GERALD O'HARA HAM STEAK ➤

| | |
|---|---|
| 1 slice ham, ½-inch thick | 1 tablespoon prepared mustard |
| 4 tablespoons maple syrup or honey | |

Place slice of ham in shallow baking pan; broil 15 minutes or until brown. Remove pan; turn ham, and spread uncooked side with mixture of mustard and maple syrup or honey. Replace under low broiler heat for about 10 minutes, watching closely so that it does not burn. Makes about 4 servings.

# ➤➤ PLANTERS' HAM AND PARSNIPS ➤

| | |
|---|---|
| 1 slice ham, 1-inch thick | ¼ cup water |
| 6 cloves | ½ cup honey |
| Nutmeg | 1 cup sliced, cooked parsnips |
| 1 cup sliced, cooked sweet potatoes | |

Dot ham with cloves; sprinkle with nutmeg, and place in greased baking pan. Pour water and honey over ham; cover and bake in moderately slow oven (325 degrees F.) for 45 minutes, or until tender. Remove from oven and cover with alternate layers of parsnips and sweet potatoes. Bake uncovered about 10 minutes or until vegetables are browned. Makes 4 to 6 servings.

# ➤➤ KIDNEY STEW ➤

| | |
|---|---|
| 2 kidneys | 1 can tomato paste OR |
| 6 slices bacon, diced | 1 can tomato soup |
| 1 onion, chopped fine | ½ cup boiling water |
| ¼ cup butter or margarine | Salt and pepper |

Split kidneys; remove fat, skin, and hard membrane. Soak in cold salt water 30 minutes. Drain; cut into small pieces, and brown lightly with bacon and onion. Add other ingredients; cover, simmer 15 minutes, until kidneys are tender. Makes 4 to 6 servings.

## ➤ GLAZING FOR HAM ➤

Roast ham
1 cup brown sugar, firmly packed
2 cups soft bread crumbs
¼ teaspoon dry mustard
¼ teaspoon paprika
¼ teaspoon black pepper
Whole cloves
1 cup mild vinegar or cider

To glaze ham, cover with mixture of brown sugar and crumbs. Mix together mustard, paprika and pepper, and sprinkle over ham. Insert cloves over top. Bake in moderately hot oven (375 degrees F.) about ½ hour or until nicely brown, basting frequently with vinegar or cider.

## ➤ MEAT LOAF ➤

1½ pounds beef, ground
½ pound pork, ground
1 large onion, chopped fine
1 teaspoon salt
⅛ teaspoon pepper
¼ green pepper, chopped fine
½ cup cracker crumbs
1 egg, beaten
½ cup milk
½ teaspoon thyme
1 can condensed tomato soup
Parsley

Mix all ingredients except thyme and soup together well; place in a greased loaf pan, or mold and place in greased pan. Bake in moderate oven (350 degrees F.) about ½ hour. Remove from oven; sprinkle thyme over loaf, and pour can of condensed tomato soup over it. Bake ½ hour longer, (basting occasionally with drippings). Garnish with parsley. Makes 6 servings.

## ➤ CREOLE SAUCE ➤

4 tablespoons chopped green pepper
1 small onion, chopped fine
2 tablespoons butter or margarine
Salt and pepper
¼ cup sliced mushrooms
2 small tomatoes, sliced
1 cup brown sauce

Simmer green pepper and onion in butter or margarine until soft. Add mushrooms and tomatoes; simmer about 5 minutes. Add brown sauce and bring to boil. Season with salt and pepper.

## ➤ BROWN SAUCE ➤

1 teaspoon grated onion
3 tablespoons butter or margarine
3 tablespoons flour
1 cup cream
1 teaspoon beef extract
Salt and pepper

Brown onion slightly in butter; stir in flour. Pour in cream gradually, stirring constantly, and cook until slightly thickened. Season with beef extract, salt, and pepper, and cook about 2 minutes longer.

# ☙ POULTRY & STUFFINGS ☙

TO MOST PEOPLE *just to say the word "South" will call to mind heaping platters of fried chicken. But it may also mean Chicken Fricassee, and Chicken with Dumplings. Or it may suggest the incomparable Brunswick Stew which is a combination of chicken (though it may be squirrel or rabbit, too,) with corn, tomatoes, lima beans, and other vegetables, and a wealth of seasonings. This is simmered a long, long time, until the flavors are intermingled and the whole makes almost a complete meal. A big iron kettleful was always found at most barbecues just as it was on that eventful barbecue day at Twelve Oaks so many years ago.*

## ➤➤ CHICKEN FRICASSEE WITH RICE ➤

| | |
|---|---|
| 1 stewing chicken, (3 pounds) | 2 slices salt pork, cut fine |
| 1 quart water | 3 tablespoons butter or margarine |
| 1 onion | 3 tablespoons flour |
| ½ bay leaf | 1½ cups stock |
| 1 teaspoon salt | ½ cup cream |
| Seasoned flour | 3 cups boiled rice |

Disjoint chicken. Cook gently with water, onion, bay leaf, and salt for 1½ to 2 hours or until tender. Remove chicken, roll in seasoned flour, fry until brown with salt pork and butter. Remove chicken, add flour to pan fat, and stir until smooth; then stir in chicken stock and cream, and simmer until thick and creamy, stirring occasionally. Season to taste. Place chicken on platter and pour gravy over it. Surround with border of boiled rice. Makes about 6 servings.

# SOUTHERN FRIED CHICKEN

Select young spring chickens about 2½ or 3 pounds each. **Dress and disjoint.** Chicken should be thoroughly chilled after dressing before it is used. Sprinkle the slightly moist chicken with well-seasoned flour. Put just a few pieces at a time, about 6, into a skillet containing 1 pound or a 1½-inch layer hot fat. Fry gently 25 to 30 minutes, turning once. Each piece is crusty brown on all sides.

## BRUNSWICK STEW

| | |
|---|---|
| 1 stewing chicken (3 to 4 pounds) | 1 or 2 onions, sliced |
| Hot water | 2 cups canned corn or cut from 8 ears |
| 1 teaspoon salt | 2 cups canned tomatoes OR |
| ⅛ teaspoon pepper | 8 fresh tomatoes |
| 4 potatoes, diced | ¼ cup butter or margarine |
| 2 cups butter beans (green limas) | ½ cup biscuit or bread crumbs |

Cut cleaned chicken; cover with boiling water, bring to a boil and simmer, covered, for about 1½ hours or until almost tender. Add seasonings after first hour of cooking. Add potatoes, butter beans and onion, and cook about 30 minutes longer. Remove bones, then add corn and tomatoes and cook until vegetables are done, adding more seasoning if desired. Add mixture of butter or margarine and crumbs, to thicken like a stew. Makes a whole meal with salad and bread. This makes a huge kettleful but is fine warmed over. Heat slowly and stir carefully to keep vegetables from breaking, especially after crumbs are added.

## OYSTER STUFFING

| | |
|---|---|
| 4 cups soft bread crumbs | ¼ teaspoon salt |
| ½ cup softened butter | ¼ teaspoon celery salt |
| 1 pint oysters | ¼ teaspoon onion salt |
| Dash paprika | |

Mix crumbs with butter; add oysters and seasonings. For 16- to 18-pound bird double the recipe.

## SOUTHERN FAVORITE PEANUT STUFFING

| | |
|---|---|
| 2 cups browned shelled peanuts | 1 egg yolk, beaten |
| 1½ cups dry bread crumbs | Stock |
| 2 tablespoons melted butter | Salt and pepper |

Grind peanuts in meat chopper and add to bread crumbs. Stir in melted butter and egg yolk. Moisten with stock from stewed giblets. Season with salt and pepper. For 10- to 12-pound turkey, make 2½ times the above amount.

# FISH & SHELLFISH

*AT THE TIME Tara and Twelve Oaks were at their height, one had to go to New Orleans or some other seaport town, where the hucksters peddled their seafoods throughout the streets—or depend on the day's catch of fresh water fish from the local rivers and streams. Now, however, it is easy to enjoy broiled oysters on the half shell, savory scalloped oysters, or frog legs, and the other specialties of that day even though we may live hundreds of miles away from the sea.*

## CREOLE BOILED FISH (Fish Bouilli)

| | |
|---|---|
| 2 to 3 pounds fish, whole or thick slices | 1 clove garlic or small onion, sliced |
| 1 quart boiling water | 1 sprig thyme |
| 1 carrot, sliced | 1 bay leaf |
| ½ cup celery leaves | 1 teaspoon salt |
| 2 tablespoons vinegar or lemon juice | |

Use a lean fish such as redfish, red snapper, halibut, pike, bass, or cod. Clean and wash whole fish thoroughly; wipe sliced fish with damp cloth. Lay sliced fish in wire basket; entwine whole fish with cord. Heat water, vegetables, and seasonings to boiling point, and simmer for 10 minutes. Add fish carefully, and simmer 10 to 20 minutes, according to thickness of fish. Fish is done when it can be pulled from bone. Remove basket of fish slices and drain, or use perforated spatula to remove whole fish. Place on hot platter; garnish as desired, serve with a fish sauce. Makes 6 servings.

## ⇥ MAMMY'S SHRIMP CAKES ⇥

1 pound fresh shrimp OR
2 cups canned shrimp
3 slices white bread, cut 1-inch thick
Hot water

2 tablespoons butter or margarine, softened
1/8 teaspoon salt
1/4 teaspoon mace
1/4 teaspoon black pepper

Drop fresh shrimp into boiling salted water, and cook 15 minutes, or until shells turn pink. Drain, and cover with cold water to chill. Drain again and remove shells, legs, and black lines running along backs. (If you use canned shrimp, rinse twice and remove black lines.) Put shrimp through food chopper. Remove crusts from bread; cover with boiling water; squeeze dry and crumble. Add butter or margarine and seasonings, and mix well with shrimp. Shape into flat cakes; place in greased shallow pan, and bake in moderate oven (350 degrees F.) about 20 minutes, turning to brown both sides. Or sauté in butter, browning both sides. Serve with an egg or cheese sauce. Makes 6 servings.

## ⇥ SOUTHERN BAKED SHAD ⇥

4 pounds shad
1/2 small onion, chopped
4 tablespoons chopped celery
1/4 cup butter or margarine
3 cups soft bread crumbs
1/2 teaspoon salt

1/8 teaspoon pepper
1 tablespoon chopped parsley
1 tablespoon chopped dill pickle
1/4 pound salt pork
Bacon fat or other fat
Salt and pepper

Select a 3- to 5-pound fish. If desired remove head and tail. Clean inside without cutting fish open along entire belly; wash thoroughly, then dry inside and outside with paper towels. Rub inside with salt. To prepare stuffing, sauté onion and celery in butter or margarine in heavy frying pan, over low heat, about 10 minutes, or until lightly browned. Then turn off heat; add bread crumbs, seasonings and chopped pickle, and toss together to mix thoroughly. Put lightly by spoonfuls into the fish. Sew edges together. Brush outside of fish with fat; sprinkle with salt and pepper. Place seam side down on greased rack in shallow baking pan. If fish is whole, curve into letter "S". Cut salt pork into 1/2-inch strips and place crosswise over back of fish. Bake uncovered in moderately hot oven (375 degrees F.) for 40 to 50 minutes, or until fish can be pushed away from back bone. Serve hot with lemon butter. Makes 6 servings.

## ➤➤ TARA SUPPER DEVILED CRABS ➤➤

| | |
|---|---|
| 4 tablespoons butter or margarine | 2 teaspoons lemon juice |
| 2 tablespoons flour | 1 teaspoon prepared mustard |
| 1 cup milk | ½ teaspoon horseradish |
| 1 teaspoon salt | 2 cups flaked crabmeat |
| 1 teaspoon chopped parsley | 2 hard-cooked eggs, chopped |
| ½ cup buttered bread crumbs | |

Melt butter or margarine; stir in flour to a smooth paste; add milk gradually, stirring constantly until mixture boils and thickens. Simmer 10 minutes. Add seasonings, crabmeat, and eggs, and mix well. Fill scallop or crab shells, or individual baking dishes with mixture. Top with bread crumbs, and bake in moderately hot oven (375 degrees F.) about 15 minutes or until crumbs are browned. Makes 6 servings.

## TIDEWATER COUNTRY FRIED SOFT-SHELL CRABS

| | |
|---|---|
| 6 soft-shell crabs | 1 egg, slightly beaten |
| Salt and pepper | 1 cup fine, dry bread crumbs |
| Fat for deep fat frying | |

Soft-shell crabs should be alive when purchased. Wash carefully to remove sand; place face down on a board. Lift the shell on each side and remove the soft, spongy substance underneath. Then turn crab face up; cut off tail, and scrape off spongy portion underneath. Wash again, and dry on paper towels. Sprinkle with salt and pepper; dip in egg, and roll in bread crumbs. Fry in hot deep fat (375 degrees F.) 3 to 4 minutes or until golden brown. Drain on unglazed paper, and serve with a tartar sauce. Makes 6 servings.

## ➤➤ TARLETON TWINS' BROILED OYSTERS ON HALF SHELL

| | |
|---|---|
| 18 oysters in shell | 2 tablespoons finely chopped parsley |
| Salt and pepper | 1 tablespoon minced onion |
| 3 strips bacon, finely chopped | ½ cup buttered bread crumbs |

Wash oyster shells and pry open, but do not pour off liquor. Sprinkle with salt and pepper. Combine bacon, parsley, and onion; sprinkle over oysters, and top with bread crumbs. Place on broiling pan and broil under medium heat 2 to 5 minutes, or until edges begin to curl. Serve hot as an appetizer. When planned for main course, increase amounts, allowing about 6 oysters per serving.

# BAKED HADDOCK WITH CELERY DRESSING

| | |
|---|---|
| 1½ to 2 pounds filet of haddock | ⅓ cup chopped parsley |
| Salt and pepper | 1 cup soft bread crumbs |
| 2 tablespoons lemon juice | ½ teaspoon sage |
| ½ cup chopped celery stalks and leaves | Hot water |
| ⅛ cup chopped onion | ¼ cup dry bread crumbs |
| 3 tablespoons butter or margarine | Paprika |

Arrange half of filets in greased shallow pan; sprinkle with salt, pepper and lemon juice. For dressing, mix together celery, onion, and butter or margarine, and heat to melt butter. Remove from heat, and add parsley, crumbs and sage. Toss to mix well; add just enough hot water to moisten slightly. Spread dressing over the fish already arranged in the pan, and cover with remaining filets. Sprinkle tops with salt, pepper, dry crumbs, and paprika. Pour ¼ cup hot water into baking dish, and bake in moderately hot oven (375 degrees F.) for 25 to 30 minutes. Serve hot. Makes 6 servings.

## ► SCALLOPED FILET OF SOLE AND SHRIMP ◄

| | |
|---|---|
| 1 to 1½ pounds of filet of sole OR | ½ teaspoon salt |
| 6 small filets | 3 tablespoons butter or margarine |
| 2½ cups hot water | 3 tablespoons flour |
| 2 tablespoons lemon juice | 1 cup canned or fresh shrimp, cooked |
| ⅔ cup buttered bread crumbs | |

Place filets in frying pan; cover with hot water, and add lemon juice and salt. Bring to a boil and simmer, covered, about 10 minutes. Remove fish to hot greased baking dish. Make sauce of butter, flour, and 2 cups of the fish stock left in frying pan. Add shrimp, and pour sauce over all. Cover with bread crumbs. Place in moderate oven (350 degrees F.) and bake about 15 minutes, or until sauce bubbles up through crumbs. Place casserole under broiler for a few minutes to brown crumbs if necessary. Makes 6 servings.

## ► FRIED FROGS' LEGS ◄

| | |
|---|---|
| 6 to 9 pair large frogs' legs | 1 egg, slightly beaten |
| Salt and pepper | 2 cups fine bread crumbs |
| 1 tablespoon lemon juice | 4 tablespoons butter |
| Parsley | |

Wash legs, and remove skin by turning it down and pulling it off like a glove. Wash and dry. Sprinkle with salt, pepper and lemon juice. Dip in egg and roll in bread crumbs. Sauté in butter about 10 to 12 minutes, or until golden brown on both sides. Makes 6 servings.

# OTHER MAIN DISHES

## PILAU, SCRAPPLE, EGGS, etc.

THE HEAVY CULTIVATION *of rice throughout the old agri-cultural south made it a staple food, along with cornmeal, hominy, and the like. And these grains crept into the delicious dishes in all the country, from the Pilaus of Charleston, to the Jambalays of New Orleans. Eggs, too, from plantation hen houses, were used with a lavish hand in omelets, soufflés, as well as in other cooking and baking such as rich cakes and whipped egg white desserts.*

### CHICKEN PILAU

1 stewing chicken (3½ pounds)          2 tablespoons butter or margarine
⅛ pound salt pork          3 cups cooked rice
1 teaspoon salt          Pepper
1 medium onion, chopped          Chopped parsley

Wash chicken; disjoint and place in large sauce pan. Cut salt pork into small pieces, and add to chicken. Cover with cold water; bring quickly to a boil; simmer, covered, 1½ to 2 hours, or until chicken is almost done. Add salt after chicken has cooked for 1 hour. Sauté onion in butter or margarine for 10 minutes, or until tender. Remove chicken from bones and mix with onion, rice, and enough chicken stock to moisten. Heat until steaming hot, seasoning with a dash of pepper and additional salt, if desired. Serve in hot dish, sprinkling chopped parsley over top. Makes 6 servings.

# ⟶ CHEESE SOUFFLÉ ⟵

| | |
|---|---|
| 4 tablespoons butter or margarine | ½ teaspoon salt |
| 4 tablespoons flour | Dash of cayenne |
| 1 cup milk | 2 to 3 drops Worcestershire Sauce |
| 1½ cups grated American cheese | 4 eggs, separated |

Melt butter or margarine and stir in flour. Add milk, stirring constantly, and cook until thickened. Remove from heat; add grated cheese and seasonings, and stir until cheese is melted. Add egg yolks, one at a time, beating thoroughly after each. Beat whites until stiff, but not dry, and fold carefully into cheese mixture. Turn into greased casserole; place in a pan of hot water, and bake in moderate oven (350 degrees F.) for 50 minutes, or until soufflé is firm and delicately browned. Serve at once. Makes 6 servings.

# ⟶ JAMBALAYA ⟵

| | |
|---|---|
| 3 cups diced, cooked chicken or turkey | ½ green pepper, chopped |
| 2 cups cooked rice | 3 tablespoons butter or margarine |
| 2 cups (No. 1 can) tomatoes | ½ teaspoon salt |
| 1 medium onion, chopped | Dash of pepper |

Use left-over chicken or turkey; mix with rice and tomatoes, and simmer for 10 minutes. Sauté onion and green pepper in butter or margarine for 5 minutes; add to rice and chicken mixture. Add salt and pepper; cover, and simmer for 30 minutes, adding hot water as needed to keep mixture moist. Stir occasionally with fork, to prevent mixture from burning, and to keep rice as whole as possible. Serve very hot. Makes 6 servings.

# ⟶ SCRAPPLE ⟵

| | |
|---|---|
| 4 hog's feet | 1 tablespoon powdered sage |
| 2 pounds fresh pork shoulder | 2⅔ cups white corn meal |
| Cold water | Fat for frying |
| 4 teaspoons salt | Flour to sprinkle |
| ¼ teaspoon pepper | |

Wash hog's feet and place with shoulder meat in a deep kettle. Cover with water. Cover pan and cook slowly for 2 hours, or until tender. Remove meat and chop fine, including all skin and fat. Measure broth. If necessary, add water to make 2 quarts. Add the chopped meat and seasonings, bring to boiling point, and stir in corn meal. Cook slowly 1 hour, stirring occasionally. Rinse loaf pans in cold water, pour in scrapple, and cool. When firm, sprinkle with flour, and brown in hot fat. Makes 6¾ pounds.

## ◄► MAMMY'S CREOLE RICE ◄►

| | |
|---|---|
| 1 large onion, sliced | 1½ cups cooked peas |
| 3 stalks celery, chopped | ½ tablespoon vinegar |
| 1½ tablespoons fat | ¼ teaspoon sugar |
| ¾ tablespoon flour | 1¼ cups cooked fresh shrimp OR |
| ¾ teaspoon salt | canned shrimp |
| ¾ cup water | 1½ tablespoons chili powder |
| 1½ cups tomatoes | 2 cups hot boiled rice |

Sauté onion and celery in fat until browned. Stir in flour and salt, and slowly add the water. Simmer 15 minutes, stirring frequently. Add tomatoes, peas, vinegar, sugar, shrimp, and chili powder, and continue cooking 10 minutes longer. Place rice in a large deep serving plate, and pour creole mixture over it. Makes 6 servings.

## ◄► CODFISH SOUFFLÉ ◄►

| | |
|---|---|
| 1 cup salt codfish | 1 tablespoon butter or margarine |
| 2 cups diced potatoes | 2 eggs, separated |
| 2 tablespoons catsup | |

Shred codfish and soak ½ hour in cold water, or prepare according to directions on package. Drain and cook with potatoes until tender. Drain; mash the potatoes; add butter or margarine and beat until light. Stir in beaten egg yolks and catsup. Fold in stiffly beaten egg whites, and turn into a greased casserole. Place in a pan of hot water and bake in a moderately hot oven (375 degrees F.) about 20 minutes. Makes 4 to 6 servings.

## ◄► PLANTATION CORN OMELET ◄►

| | |
|---|---|
| 4 eggs, separated | ½ teaspoon salt |
| 2 cups (12-ounce can) whole kernel | Dash of pepper |
| corn, chopped fine | ½ cup light cream |
| 2 tablespoons butter or margarine | |

Beat egg yolks until thick and lemon colored; add corn, seasonings and cream. Fold in stiffly beaten egg whites. Melt butter or margarine in frying pan; pour in egg mixture, and cook slowly over low heat. When omelet is brown on the bottom, place in a moderate oven (350 degrees F.) and bake 10 to 15 minutes or until firm on top. Remove from oven; fold and serve immediately. Makes 6 servings.

## ➤➤ EGG PILAU ➤➤

1½ cups rice
4 cups chicken broth or stock
1 teaspoon salt
Dash of pepper

⅛ teaspoon onion salt
1 tablespoon chopped parsley
4 tablespoons butter or margarine
4 eggs, slightly beaten

Wash rice thoroughly; drain. Place chicken stock or broth and salt in deep kettle; heat to boiling point. Add rice slowly. Cook, covered, for 20 minutes, or until rice is tender. The rice should absorb all of the liquid. Add seasonings, butter or margarine, slightly beaten eggs. Beat 2 minues, serve at once. Makes 6 servings.

## ➤➤ SAVORY HOMINY WITH CANADIAN BACON ➤➤

3 cups milk
2 eggs
1 cup granulated hominy
1 teaspoon salt

1½ tablespoons onion juice
3 tablespoons finely chopped
green pepper
12 thin slices Canadian bacon, broiled

Beat milk and eggs slightly; stir in hominy, salt, onion juice, and green pepper. Pour into greased casserole and place in pan of hot water. Bake in moderate oven (350 degrees F.) for 1 to 1½ hours, or until hominy is soft. Stir occasionally during first part of cooking. Serve with broiled Canadian bacon. Makes 6 servings.

## ➤➤ SCALLOPED NOODLES WITH CHICKEN ➤➤

3 cups cooked noodles
3 cups diced, cooked chicken
¼ pound mushrooms, sliced
½ teaspoon salt

Dash of pepper
2 tablespoons melted butter or
margarine
1 cup hot chicken broth

½ cup buttered bread crumbs

Place half the noodles in a greased baking dish; add half the chicken and mushrooms. Repeat layers, alternating noodles, chicken and mushrooms. Mix the salt, pepper, and butter or margarine, with the hot chicken broth. Pour in filled casserole. Cover with bread crumbs and bake uncovered in a moderate oven (350 degrees F.) about 20 minutes or until brown. Makes 6 servings.

## ➤➤ MELANIE'S SHIRRED EGGS WITH HAM ➤➤

6 eggs
Salt and pepper
2 tablespoons butter or margarine

6 tablespoons finely chopped
cooked ham
1 tablespoon chopped parsley

Break the eggs into individual greased ramekins. Add a dash of salt and pepper, and dot with butter or margarine. Sprinkle with chopped ham and parsley. Bake in a moderate oven (350 degrees F.) for 15 minutes, or until eggs are firm. Makes 6 servings.

# ❁ SOUTHERN BREADS ❁

EXCEPT IN CRUELLY *troubled times, no meal at Tara (or any Southern homestead) was complete without hot breads, served piping hot and dripping with butter. The hot breads varied. They might be popovers, Sally Lunns, Muffins, Hoe Cakes, Spoon Bread, or the Cracklin' Bread famed in song and story. And these were on the table bright and early in the morning, too. Mrs. Mary Randolph in her famous book, "The Virginia Housewife or Methodical Cookbook", published in 1838, instructed her fellow housewives to "begin the day with an early breakfast, requiring each person to take their seats when the muffins, buckwheat cakes, etc., are placed on the table. This looks social and comfortable".*

## ➤ "CHURNING DAY" BUTTERMILK BISCUITS ◄

| | |
|---|---|
| 2 cups sifted flour | ½ teaspoon baking soda |
| 1 teaspoon salt | ⅓ cup shortening |
| 2 teaspoons baking powder | ¾ cup buttermilk |
| 1 tablespoon melted fat | |

Sift flour, salt, baking powder, and soda together into mixing bowl. Cut in shortening until mixture resembles coarse crumbs. Add buttermilk all at once, and stir just until dough follows fork around bowl. Pat out ¼ or ½-inch thick on lightly floured board, and cut with biscuit cutter. Place on greased baking sheet; brush lightly with melted fat, and bake in a very hot oven (450 degrees F.) about 15 minutes. Makes 16 medium-size tall biscuits.

## ►◄ MELANIE'S POPOVERS ►◄

| | |
|---|---|
| 1 cup sifted flour | 1 cup milk |
| ½ teaspoon salt | 1 tablespoon melted butter or |
| 2 eggs | margarine, or salad oil |

Sift flour and salt together into mixing bowl. Beat eggs until light and thick. Stir in flour and ⅓ of milk; continue to beat slowly until all flour is moistened—about 30 seconds. Add remaining milk and liquid fat gradually, beating until mixture is free from lumps, 1 to 2 minutes. Pour into greased baking cups, filling them a little less than half-full. Iron, oven-glass or earthenware cups may be used. Bake in hot oven (425 degrees F.) about 40 minutes. Makes 8 popovers.

## ►◄ HOME STYLE CORNBREAD ►◄

| | |
|---|---|
| 1 cup sifted flour | ½ teaspoon salt |
| 1 cup cornmeal, yellow preferred | 3 tablespoons sugar |
| 2 teaspoons baking powder | 1 egg |
| ½ teaspoon baking soda | 1 cup sour milk or buttermilk |
| 4 tablespoons melted shortening | |

Sift flour, cornmeal, baking powder, soda, and salt together into mixing bowl. Combine sugar and egg; beat until light. Add sour milk or buttermilk, and shortening. Combine slowly with dry ingredients. If milk is quite thick, a little more may be needed to thin batter. Stir only until ingredients are mixed. Grease pan (9" x 9" x 2") generously, and cover with thick sprinkling of cornmeal. Pour batter in pan, and bake in hot oven (425 degrees F.) about 25 minutes, or until nicely browned.

## ►◄ MASTER RECIPE FOR BISCUIT SHORTCAKE ►◄

| | |
|---|---|
| 2 cups sifted flour | ½ teaspoon salt |
| 8 teaspoons baking powder | 6 to 8 tablespoons shortening |
| ⅓ to ⅔ cup milk | |

Sift flour, baking powder, and salt together into mixing bowl. Cut in shortening with 2 knives, pastry blender or finger-tips. When using fingers, pick up mixture and rub shortening in quickly; drop and take up another portion. Repeat until mixing is complete. Mix only until the mass resembles cornmeal. Make a little well in center; pour into this well most of the milk at once, stirring with a fork or spoon. The amount of liquid needed varies with the flour, but add it until the mixture follows the spoon or fork in the bowl. Mix no longer than needed. The ideal is a soft dough that may be handled. Remove ball of dough to a lightly floured board; knead lightly 10 to 20 times; roll to ¼-inch thickness. Cut in large (8-inch) rounds, or in individual size rounds, and place on greased baking sheet. Two rounds may be put together like sandwiches, spreading melted butter or margarine between and on top before baking. Bake in very hot oven (450 degrees F.) 12 to 15 minutes. Remove from oven, separate biscuit layers and put filling between layers and on top.

### Tomato Variation

Follow master recipe for Biscuit Shortcake. Substitute tomato juice for milk. About 1 cup will be required, the exact amount depending on the consistency of the juice and the flour. The biscuit is tinted attractively, and is fine for meat shortcake.

### Sweet Variation

Follow master recipe for Biscuit Shortcake. Add from 3 tablespoons to ½ cup sugar with dry ingredients, according to preference. One beaten egg sometimes is added with the milk (½ cup), but the biscuit may not be as flaky. Use with strawberries, peaches or other fruit.

## ⟶ SUNDAY NIGHT PLAIN MUFFINS ⟶

| | |
|---|---|
| 2 cups sifted flour | 2 tablespoons sugar |
| 3 teaspoons baking powder | 1 egg, well beaten |
| ½ teaspoon salt | 1 cup milk |

2 tablespoons melted butter or margarine

Sift flour, baking powder, salt and sugar together into mixing bowl. Combine egg, milk and butter or margarine, and add to dry mixture as quickly as possible, mixing only enough to dampen flour. Drop by spoonfuls in greased muffin pans, and bake in hot oven (400-425 degrees F.) 25 minutes. Makes 12 muffins.

*Berry Muffins:* Reserve ¼ cup flour; use to dredge 1 cup fresh blueberries and add to mixture after liquid. Amount of sugar may be doubled.

*Date or Raisin Muffins:* Add ½ to 1 cup sliced, pitted dates or raisins.

[ 23 ]

# ➤ SALLY LUNN ➤

| | |
|---|---|
| 2 eggs, separated | ½ teaspoon nutmeg |
| ½ cup sugar | ¾ cup milk |
| 2 cups sifted flour | 1 tablespoon melted butter or |
| 2 teaspoons baking powder | margarine, or salad oil |
| ½ teaspoon salt | |

Beat egg yolks; add sugar. Sift dry ingredients together, and add alternately with milk to egg and sugar mixture. Then add melted butter or margarine. Beat until smooth. Beat egg whites until stiff but not dry, and fold them in. Pour in a well-greased square pan or in muffin pans. Bake squares in moderate oven (350 degrees F.) about 40 minutes. Bake muffins in moderately hot oven (375 degrees F.) about 25 minutes. Makes 16 squares or 12 muffins.

# ➤ AUNT PITTYPAT'S CREAM SCONES ➤

| | |
|---|---|
| 2 cups sifted flour | ½ teaspoon salt |
| 4 tablespoons baking powder | 4 tablespoons butter or margarine |
| 2 teaspoons sugar | 2 eggs |
| ⅓ cup cream or milk | |

Sift dry ingredients together into mixing bowl. Work in butter or margarine with pastry blender, fork, or finger tips. Separate eggs (reserving a small amount of unbeaten white for glaze later). Beat rest of eggs well, add cream or milk, and stir into dry ingredients. Toss on floured board, pat, and roll ¾-inch thick. Cut in squares, diamonds, or triangles. Brush with reserved egg white diluted with 1 teaspoon water. Sprinkle with sugar, and bake in very hot oven (450 degrees F.) for 15 minutes. Makes 12 scones.

# ➤ CRACKLIN' BREAD ➤

| | |
|---|---|
| 2 cups cornmeal | 2½ cups sweet milk |
| 1 cup boiling water | 1 teaspoon salt |
| 1 tablespoon shortening | 2 teaspoons baking powder |
| 2 eggs | 1 cup broken cracklings |

Scald cornmeal with boiling water; add shortening and cool slightly. Beat eggs thoroughly; add milk and salt. Combine the two mixtures. Add the baking powder and cracklings and blend thoroughly. Turn into a well-greased pan, and bake in a moderately hot oven (375 degrees F.) for 25 to 30 minutes. Makes 6 servings.

(Cracklings are small pieces of pork fat which have been fried until all grease has been extracted.)

# ATLANTA WAFFLES

| | |
|---|---|
| 1½ cups sifted flour | 1 cup milk (about) |
| 3 teaspoons baking powder | 2 egg yolks, well beaten |
| ½ teaspoon salt | 3 to 4 tablespoons melted butter or |
| 2 teaspoons sugar | margarine |

2 egg whites, beaten stiff

Sift dry ingredients together into mixing bowl. Stir in milk gradually, then egg yolks and butter or margarine. Finally fold in egg whites. Bake in a moderately hot waffle baker 4 to 5 minutes. Makes 6 to 8 waffles.

# POTATO FLOUR MUFFINS

| | |
|---|---|
| 3 eggs, separated | 2 tablespoons cold water |
| ⅛ teaspoon salt | 1 teaspoon baking powder |
| 2 tablespoons sugar | ½ cup sifted potato flour |

Beat egg yolks; stir in salt, sugar, and water. Sift baking powder and flour together, and stir into first mixture. Fold in fluffy beaten egg whites. Bake in moderate oven (350 degrees F.) 25 to 30 minutes. Makes 12 medium-size muffins. (These are like delicate sponge cakes but are not as sweet in flavor.)

# COFFEECAKE WHEELS

| | |
|---|---|
| 1 cup butter or margarine | 4½ cups sifted flour |
| ½ cup granulated sugar | ¼ cup melted butter or margarine |
| ½ teaspoon salt | ¼ cup brown sugar |
| 2 tablespoons grated lemon rind | ¾ cup seedless raisins |
| 2 eggs, well beaten | ¾ cup chopped walnut meats |
| 1 compressed yeast cake | 6 tablespoons granulated sugar |
| 1 cup light sour cream | 1½ teaspoons cinnamon |

Cream butter or margarine gradually; add granulated sugar, and cream thoroughly. Add salt, lemon rind, eggs, and yeast cake, which has been dissolved in the sour cream. Blend well. Add flour and mix thoroughly. Cover, and chill in the refrigerator for 3 hours. Remove from refrigerator and let rise for 1½ hours. Then roll dough on a lightly floured board to about ¼-inch thickness. Cover bottom of a 9" x 12" pan with melted butter and brown sugar. Spread the surface of the dough with the remaining ingredients, which have been mixed together. Roll up as you would a jelly roll, pressing edges together. Cut crosswise into slices ¾-inch thick. Arrange slices on top of butter and brown sugar mixture. Cover with a clean cloth and let rise in a warm place (75 to 85 degrees F.) about ½ hour, or until light. Bake in a moderately hot oven (375 degrees F.) 35 minutes. Serve warm. Makes 20 coffeecake wheels.

## ➤➤ DIXIE SPOON BREAD ➤➤

| | |
|---|---|
| 3 cups milk, scalded | 1 teaspoon sugar |
| 1 cup white cornmeal | 1 teaspoon salt |
| 1 teaspoon melted butter or | 3 egg yolks, beaten |
|    margarine | 3 egg whites, stiffly beaten |

Add scalded milk gradually to cornmeal, and cook 5 minutes, stirring constantly. Add butter or margarine, sugar, and salt. Add beaten egg yolks; beat well; then fold in beaten egg whites. Turn into greased baking dish, and bake in a moderate oven (350 degrees F.) for 45 to 50 minutes. Serve hot from baking dish with plenty of butter. Make 4 or 5 servings.

## ➤➤ BAKING POWDER BISCUITS ➤➤

| | |
|---|---|
| 2 cups sifted flour | 1 teaspoon salt |
| 4 teaspoons baking powder | 4 tablespoons shortening |
| ¾ cup milk (about) | |

Sift flour, baking powder, and salt together into mixing bowl. Cut in shortening until mixture resembles coarse cornmeal. Make a well in center and pour in liquid. Toss flour into this with fork, stirring half a dozen times around edge of bowl. When coarse particles barely adhere, turn out on lightly floured board or on a pastry cloth. Knead lightly for a few seconds with folding motion. This helps dough to rise straight, and produces flaky delicate biscuits that break apart in layers. Pat or roll out dough ¼ to ½-inch thick as desired. (Southern biscuits are usually thin and crusty.) Biscuits double in height in baking. Cut in rounds 1½ to 2 inches in diameter. Place one inch apart on greased baking sheet. Bake in very hot oven (450 degrees F.) 8 to 10 minutes for thin biscuits, 12 to 15 minutes for tall biscuits. Makes about 15 tall biscuits.

*Variations*—Follow above recipe, and add to dry ingredients:

1. *Cheese.* Add ½ cup grated American cheese.
2. *Herb.* Add 1 tablespoon minced parsley and 1 tablespoon chopped chives.
3. *Ham.* Add ½ cup finely chopped cooked ham.

## ➤➤ LACY CORN CAKES ➤➤

| | |
|---|---|
| 2 eggs | 1 teaspoon salt |
| 2 cups milk | 4 tablespoons melted butter or |
| 1⅛ cups cornmeal |    margarine, or salad oil |

Beat eggs until light; add milk. Slowly add cornmeal and salt; mix well. Add butter or margarine. Drop by spoonfuls on hot well-greased griddle; stir batter each time a spoonful is taken out. Brown on one side, then on the other. Makes about 40 paper-thin cakes.

# ⮫ VEGETABLES ⮬

BESIDES THE SWEET *potatoes, or yams, okra, and collards of the southland, there are numerous other ways of pre-paring vegetables "Southern Style" to be remembered. The following recipe from a cook book,* The Frugal Housewife or Complete Woman Cook, *was written by Sussanah Carter about 1796. "TO STEW CUCUMBERS: Pare twelve cucum-bers, and slice them as thick as a crownpiece; put them to drain, and lay them in a coarse cloth till they are dry; flour them and fry them brown in butter, cut out the fat, then put to them some gravy, a little port wine, some pepper, cloves, and mace; let them stew a little; then roll a bit of butter in flour, and toss them up; season with salt."*

## ⭢ CORN FRITTERS ⭠

| | |
|---|---|
| 1 cup sifted flour | 1 tablespoon melted shortening |
| 1 teaspoon baking powder | ½ cup milk |
| ½ teaspoon salt | 2 cups (12-ounce can) whole |
| ¼ teaspoon sugar | kernel corn, drained |
| 1 egg, slightly beaten | Fat for deep fat frying |

Mix and sift flour, baking powder, salt, and sugar. Beat egg, melted shortening and milk together with a rotary egg beater. Add corn, and combine with dry ingredients, mixing well. Drop by spoonfuls into hot deep fat (365 degrees F.) and fry 3 to 5 minutes, or until golden brown. Drain on unglazed paper. Serve piping hot as vegetable, or serve as luncheon dish, with maple syrup and crisp bacon curls. Makes about 12 fritters and serves 6.

## ⇤ FRIED EGGPLANT or SUMMER SQUASH ⇥

1 eggplant OR
1 pound Summer squash

Seasoned flour OR
Fine bread crumbs

Butter or bacon fat

Wash eggplant; pare and cut in ½-inch slices. Or wash squash, and cut crosswise in slices. Dip slices in well-seasoned flour or crumbs, and sauté slowly in fat for 10 to 15 minutes, or until crisp and browned, turning occasionally. Serve hot. Makes 6 servings.

## ⇤ BOILED OKRA ⇥

1½ pounds okra
Water to cover
½ teaspoon salt

2 to 3 tablespoons butter
Pepper
Vinegar, if desired

Use young, tender and crisp pods from 2 to 4 inches long. Wash; remove stems; leave small pods whole, or cut all pods crosswise in ½-inch slices. Cook, uncovered, in boiling salted water to cover for 15 to 25 minutes, or until just tender. Drain; and butter, and season to taste with salt and pepper. Makes 6 servings.

## ⇤ CANDIED YAMS ⇥

6 small yams
¼ cup honey

¼ cup brown sugar
¼ cup butter or margarine

¼ cup hot water

Cook yams in boiling salted water; peel and cut in halves lengthwise. Place pieces in greased baking dish. Cook honey, sugar, butter or margarine, and hot water together for 5 minutes. Pour syrup over yams and bake in a moderately hot oven (375 degrees F.) about 20 minutes, or until browned. Makes 6 servings.

## ⇤ SWEET POTATO FRITTERS ⇥

2 cups mashed, cooked
sweet potatoes
2 tablespoons melted butter
or margarine
2 eggs, separated

1 cup milk
½ cup flour
1 teaspoon baking powder
1 tablespoon sugar
½ teaspoon salt

Fat for deep fat frying

Mix together potatoes, butter or margarine, egg yolks, and milk. Mix and sift flour, baking powder, sugar, and salt; stir into potato mixture. Fold in stiffly beaten egg whites. Drop by spoonfuls into hot deep fat (365 degrees F.) and fry for 2 to 4 minutes, or until golden brown. Drain on unglazed paper. Serve hot. Makes 18 to 24 fritters and serves 6.

# ✌ SALADS ✌

SALADS IN THE *southern tongue, always speak with a Creole accent. The common New Orleans practice was for each person to mix his own fresh green salad at the table.*

## ➤ FRENCH DRESSING ➤

½ cup salad oil
2 tablespoons vinegar or
   lemon juice
½ teaspoon salt

Pinch or sugar (optional)
½ teaspoon dry mustard
½ teaspoon paprika
1 small clove of garlic (if desired)

Measure ingredients into bottle or jar, and shake thoroughly just before using. For garlic flavor, crush clove of garlic with fork; add salt and oil and let stand 10 minutes or longer. Drain to remove garlic and add oil to bottle.

## ➤ ROQUEFORT FRENCH DRESSING ➤

Mix cheese with French dressing just before serving.

## ➤ FRESH VEGETABLE SALAD BOWL ➤

1 cup finely sliced raw cauliflower
2 medium tomatoes, cut in wedges
½ cup sliced radishes
1 cup chopped celery
¼ cup finely chopped onion
1 cup diced cucumber

½ head lettuce
1 stalk French endive
1 cup small cubes American cheese
   OR Swiss cheese OR
¼ cup Roquefort cheese
   French dressing

Prepare vegetables and cheese, and chill in refrigerator for several hours. Just before serving, break lettuce into 1½-inch pieces, and separate the endive. Toss all ingredients together lightly in a large salad bowl. Sprinkle well-shaken French dressing over mixture, and turn pieces over gently. Makes 6 servings.

## ➤ FRUIT SALAD BOWL ➤

| | |
|---|---|
| 1 grapefruit | 1 head lettuce |
| 2 oranges | ½ bunch watercress |
| 12 pitted dates or cooked prunes | 1 package (3-ounce) cream cheese, |
| ¼ cup chopped preserved ginger | cubed |

French dressing

Pare grapefruit and oranges; cut along membranes of each section and lift out section. Prepare other fruits, lettuce, watercress and cheese. Chill several hours. Just before serving, break up lettuce into 1½-inch pieces into a large salad bowl; add watercress and fruits tossing lightly. Sprinkle with well-mixed French dressing, and toss together carefully, adding cheese toward end of mixing. Serve from bowl on chilled salad plates. Makes 6 servings.

## ➤ PEACHSTREET CRABFLAKE SALAD ➤

| | |
|---|---|
| 2 cups (2 No. 1 cans) crabmeat | 3 tablespoons mayonnaise |
| 2 tablespoons grated onion | ½ teaspoon Worcestershire sauce |
| 2 small carrots, grated | Paprika |
| 9 tablespoons salad oil | Celery Salt |
| 3 tablespoons vinegar | Cayenne |

Crisp lettuce or romaine

Flake crabmeat, removing any bone. Add onions and carrots. Shake together in a bottle salad oil, vinegar, mayonnaise and seasonings, adding enough paprika to give a pink tinge to dressing. Add dressing to salad mixture; toss together lightly, and chill ½ hour or longer. Serve on crisp lettuce or romaine on chilled salad plates. Makes 6 servings.

## ➤ GREEN SALAD BOWL ➤

| | |
|---|---|
| Lettuce | Tender spinach leaves |
| Curly endive | Tender dandelion greens |
| Chicory or French endive | Radishes |
| Watercress | Cucumber |

Use several or all of greens, selecting young, tender ones. Remove all wilted leaves, and wash thoroughly; drain. Roll in a cloth and place in refrigerator to crisp, for several hours. Just before serving, rub chilled bowl with garlic, if desired. Break greens with fingers into 1½-inch pieces into bowl. Cut radishes crosswise in thin slices. Cut cucumbers in thin slices or cubes, leaving green rind on, if desired. Toss together lightly. Add French dressing and toss lightly.

# CAKES, FROSTING & COOKIES

MOST HOUSEWIVES, *starting the day's meals, do not meas-ure out the vast quantities of eggs, butter and flour as Ellen did to Cookie each morning in the smokehouse at Tara. We buy them as needed at the corner grocery store, but we still like to make and eat the Lady Baltimore Cake with its high, white frosting and filled with figs, raisins and nuts. Our men folks will still smack their lips over these rich fruit and pound cakes.*

## ◆→ BROWN SUGAR MERINGUE SPICE CAKE ←◆

| | |
|---|---|
| 1⅛ cups sifted cake flour | ¼ teaspoon salt |
| ½ teaspoon baking soda | ½ cup shortening |
| ½ teaspoon baking powder | 1½ cups brown sugar |
| ⅛ teaspoon ground cloves | 2 eggs |
| ½ teaspoon cinnamon | ½ cup sour milk or buttermilk |

¼ cup broken nutmeats

Sift flour, soda, baking powder, cloves, cinnamon, and salt to-gether. Cream the shortening until soft; gradually add one cup of the brown sugar; continue to cream until light and fluffy. Beat one whole egg and one egg yolk until light; add to sugar mixture, and beat thoroughly. Add sifted dry ingredients to mixture alternately with the sour milk, beating after each addition until smooth. Turn into greased and lightly floured loaf pan (8″ x 8″ x 2″). Spread with a meringue made as follows: Beat the remaining one egg white until quite stiff; gradually add remaining ½ cup brown sugar, continuing to beat, using either a hand beater or an electric beater at high speed. Then sprinkle with nutmeats, and bake in a moderate oven (350 degrees F.) for 50 minutes.

# MELANIE'S HONEY-NOUGAT ICING

2 egg whites, unbeaten
1½ cups granulated sugar
4 tablespoons cold water
2 tablespoons white corn syrup
2 tablespoons honey
¼ teaspoon cream of tartar
⅛ teaspoon salt
½ teaspoon vanilla extract
¼ cup chopped, toasted almonds or other nuts

Combine first 7 ingredients in top of double boiler, and stir gently until well mixed. Place over rapidly boiling water, and beat constantly with a rotary egg beater until the mixture peaks from the end of the beater (about 7 minutes). Then remove from heat; add vanilla, and beat until thick enough to spread. Sprinkle nuts on sides or top of cake. Fills and frosts 2 (9-inch) layers.

# PECAN COOKIES

1 cup sifted all-purpose flour
⅛ teaspoon cream of tartar
½ cup shortening
⅔ cup brown sugar
1 egg, beaten
⅓ cup chopped pecan meats

Sift flour with cream of tartar. Cream the shortening; gradually add brown sugar and blend well. Then add egg and mix thoroughly. Add dry ingredients with nut meats to the creamed mixture; beat until smooth. Drop by level teaspoonfuls on to greased or oiled baking pans, and bake in slow oven (300 degrees F.) for 12 to 14 minutes. Remove with a spatula while hot. Makes 48 cookies.

# SOUTHERN SOUR CREAM COOKIES

1⅔ cups sifted cake flour
1 teaspoon baking powder
¼ teaspoon baking soda
½ teaspoon salt
⅓ cup shortening
⅔ cup granulated sugar
1 egg
½ cup light sour cream
½ cup chopped nutmeats
¼ teaspoon cinnamon
1 tablespoon granulated sugar

Sift flour, baking powder, soda, and salt together. Cream the shortening well; gradually add the ⅔ cup sugar, beating after each addition until mixture is light and fluffy. Add egg and beat thoroughly. Add sifted dry ingredients alternately with sour cream; beat until smooth after each addition. Stir in chopped nutmeats, and drop by teaspoonfuls on a greased or oiled baking sheet. Press each cookie somewhat flat with the bottom of a glass dipped in additional granulated sugar. Sprinkle tops of cookies with cinnamon and 1 tablespoon sugar mixed together. Bake in hot oven (400 degrees F.) 10 to 12 minutes. Makes 3 dozen cookies.

## ━━ SEVEN MINUTE ICING ━━

2 egg whites
1½ cups granulated or powdered
   sugar

1 tablespoon white corn syrup
5 tablespoons water
½ teaspoon vanilla extract

Put all ingredients except vanilla in top of double boiler. Have water in bottom part of boiler boiling rapidly. Stir the mixture until sugar is dissolved (about 1 minute), then let cook 2 minutes without stirring. Now remove double boiler from range, and beat icing over hot water with rotary beater or electric beater at high speed for about 7 minutes, or until it holds its shape. Add vanilla and beat 1 minute. Fills and frosts 2-layer cake 9" in diameter.

## ━━ PITTYPAT'S CARAMEL ICING ━━

1½ cups dark-brown sugar, firmly
   packed

1½ cups granulated sugar
1½ cups milk

2 tablespoons butter or margarine

Combine sugars and milk and bring to boil, stirring gently. Boil without stirring to 232 degrees F., or until a little mixture forms a very soft ball in cold water. Add butter or margarine, remove from heat, and cool to 110 degrees F. (lukewarm). Then with a spoon or electric beater at medium speed, beat until thick, creamy, and of consistency to spread. If necessary, place over hot water to keep soft while spreading, or beat in a little top milk. Fills and frosts 2-layer cake 9" in diameter, or frosts an 8" x 8" x 2" cake.

## ━━ PEACHTREE STREET GINGERBREAD CAKE ━━

2½ cups sifted cake flour
1½ teaspoons baking soda
½ teaspoon ground cloves
1 teaspoon cinnamon
1 teaspoon ginger

½ teaspoon salt
½ cup shortening
½ cup granulated sugar
1 egg, well beaten
1 cup molasses

1 cup hot water

Sift flour, soda, spices and salt together. Cream the shortening; gradually add sugar, and cream well. Add beaten egg and the molasses; blend thoroughly. Stir in sifted dry ingredients alternately with hot water. Beat until smooth after each addition. Pour into greased shallow pan (9" x 9" x 1½") and bake in a moderate oven (350 degrees F.) for 45 to 50 minutes. Or turn into greased and floured cup cake pans and bake in a moderately hot oven (375 degrees F.) for 20 to 30 minutes. Makes about 2 dozen cup cakes.

## ━━◆ WHITE POUND CAKE ◆━━

| | |
|---|---|
| 4 cups sifted cake flour | 2 teaspoons vanilla extract |
| ¾ teaspoon baking powder | 1 teaspoon almond extract |
| 1¼ cups shortening | 2 cups granulated sugar |
| ⅛ cup butter or margarine | 1¾ cups egg whites, unbeaten |
| 1¼ teaspoons salt | ½ cup candied cherries, cut fine |
| ¼ cup chopped citron or angelica | |

Sift flour and baking powder together. Cream the shortening, butter or margarine, salt, and vanilla and almond extracts. Gradually add sugar, continuing to cream until light and fluffy. Add unbeaten egg whites in fifths, creaming thoroughly after each addition. Fold dry ingredients into creamed mixture in fourths, then stir in cherries and citron. Arrange in two greased paper-lined loaf pans (10″ x 5″ x 3″) and bake in a moderate oven (325 degrees F.) about 1½ hours.

## ━━◆ DELICIOUS NUT CAKE ◆━━

| | |
|---|---|
| 2 cups sifted cake flour | 1 cup granulated sugar |
| 2 teaspoons baking powder | 1 egg |
| ¼ teaspoon salt | 1 cup chopped walnut meats |
| 4 tablespoons shortening | ¾ cup milk |
| 1 teaspoon vanilla extract | |

Sift flour and baking powder together. Cream the shortening, the shortening thoroughly, add sugar gradually, continuing to cream until light and fluffy. Add egg and beat thoroughly. Add nuts. Stir in dry ingredients alternately with milk, to which vanilla extract has been added, small amount at a time. Beat after each addition until smooth. Pour in greased square pan, (8″ x 8″ x 2″), and bake in a moderate oven (350 degrees F.) for 50 minutes. Or bake in a greased loaf pan (8″ x 4½″ x 3½″) in a moderate oven (350 degrees F.) 1¼ hours. Spread with Honey-Nougat (page 32).

## ━━◆ LADY BALTIMORE CAKE ◆━━

| | |
|---|---|
| 2 cups sifted cake flour | 1⅓ cups granulated sugar |
| 2½ teaspoons baking powder | 1 teaspoon vanilla extract |
| ½ teaspoon salt | ⅔ cup milk |
| ½ cup shortening | 5 egg whites |

Sift flour, baking powder and salt together. Cream the shortening until light. Gradually add sugar, continuing to cream until light and fluffy. Add dry ingredients alternately with combined vanilla extract and milk, beating after each addition until smooth. Fold in stiffly beaten egg whites. Pour batter into three greased

8-inch layer-cake pans, and bake in moderately hot oven (375 degrees F.) for 25 to 30 minutes. After removing layers from oven, set them on cake racks, remove pans, and turn cake layers right side up. When cool, fill and frost with Lady Baltimore Frosting and Filling (below).

## LADY BALTIMORE FROSTING AND FILLING

| | |
|---|---|
| 1⅔ cups granulated sugar | ⅓ teaspoon cream of tartar |
| ½ cup water | ½ cup egg whites |

Combine sugar, water, and cream of tartar; stir until smooth. If day is clear, cook without stirring to 260 degrees F., or to the hardball stage. Cook to 270 degrees F. if day is cloudy. If crystals appear on inside of pan, wipe them down with a damp cloth. Meanwhile beat egg whites in large bowl until stiff. Then pour the sugar syrup gradually, while beating, over stiffly beaten egg whites, and beat until mixture peaks or pulls away from sides of bowl. Divide mixtures into halves. Into one half fold the following:

| | |
|---|---|
| ⅛ cup chopped nutmeats | 1 teaspoon vanilla extract |
| ½ cup chopped seeded raisins | 1 tablespoon chopped candied cherries |
| 2 dried figs, cut into thin strips | |

Fill the three layers of Lady Baltimore Cake (page 34), with this mixture. Spread top with remaining frosting. Garnish with cherries and nutmeats.

## ━━➤ SILVER TEA CAKES ◄━━

| | |
|---|---|
| 2 cups sifted cake flour | 1 cup granulated sugar |
| 5 teaspoons baking powder | 4 egg whites, unbeaten |
| ½ cup shortening | 1¼ teaspoons vanilla extract |

Sift flour, baking powder, and salt together. Cream the shortening. Gradually add sugar, continuing to cream until light and fluffy. Add egg whites a little at a time, and beat thoroughly after each addition. Add dry ingredients alternately with combined milk and vanilla extract; beat until smooth after each addition. Turn into a large shallow pan (about 10″ x 16″ x 2″), lined with waxed paper. Bake in moderately hot oven (375 degrees F.) for 25 minutes. Let stand 5 minutes; then turn from pan and remove waxed paper. Frost with Seven-Minute Icing (page 33) or dust with powdered sugar, then cut into squares. Makes about 30 fancy cakes.

# TARA FRUIT CAKE

| | |
|---|---|
| 1 pound white raisins | ¼ teaspoon salt |
| ½ pound citron | 2 teaspoons baking powder |
| 1 pound candied pineapple | 1 cup shortening |
| 1 pound candied cherries | 1 cup granulated sugar |
| ¼ pound mixed orange and lemon peel | 5 eggs |
| 1 pound nutmeats | ¼ cup fruit juice |
| 3 cups sifted all-purpose flour | 1½ tablespoons vanilla extract |

Cut up fruit and nuts coarsely, and mix thoroughly with one cup of the flour. Sift remaining two cups of flour, salt, and baking powder together. Cream the shortening; gradually add sugar, and cream well. Add eggs, one at a time, beating vigorously after each addition. Stir in sifted dry ingredients alternately with combined fruit juice and vanilla extract. Fold in floured fruits and nutmeats. Pour into two loaf pans about 5½" x 9½" x 2¾", which have been greased and lined with heavy waxed paper. Bake in slow oven (300 degrees F.) for 2¼ to 2½ hours. Makes about six pounds.

# CHOCOLATE FRUIT CAKE

| | |
|---|---|
| 1½ cups sifted all-purpose flour | 1 cup granulated sugar |
| 1½ teaspoons baking powder | ¼ pound semi-sweet chocolate |
| ¼ teaspoon salt | 2 cups coarsely chopped walnut meats |
| 3 eggs, well beaten | 1 cup coarsely cut-up dates |
| 1 cup halved candied cherries | |

Sift flour, baking powder, and salt together. Combine eggs and sugar; beat well with spoon. Cut the chocolate into pieces about the size of lima beans; add with nuts and fruits to flour mixture. Fold in egg mixture. Pour into greased loaf pan (9½" x 5½" x 2¾") with bottom lined with waxed paper. Bake in moderate oven (325 degrees F.) for 1½ hours. (No liquid is needed in this recipe.)

# JUDY CHOCOLATE ICING

| | |
|---|---|
| 1 cup sifted confectioners' sugar | ½ teaspoon vanilla extract |
| 1 egg or 2 egg yolks, unbeaten | 4 squares (4-ounces) unsweetened |
| ¼ cup milk | chocolate, melted |
| 1 tablespoon softened butter or margarine | |

Combine ingredients in order given. Then beat with a rotary egg beater or electric beater at medium speed, until stiff enough to spread (about 5 minutes). Fills and frosts 2 (9-inch) layers or frosts an 8" x 8" x 2" cake. Delicious with chopped walnuts sprinkled on sides of cake.

# ⌒ DESSERTS ⌒

CERTAINLY THE RICH, *toothsome desserts of the South have always seemed irreconcilable to the seventeen-inch waistlines claimed by the ladies. But there they were: Syllabub, bursting with whipped cream, egg white, sugar and sherry; Pecan Pie with brown sugar, syrup, eggs and pecans; not to mention Trifles, steaming Plum Pudding, and Hard Sauce. And there, too, according to stories, were the seventeen-inch waists. We are fortunate, however, in other ways. It may have been necessary to send all the way from Tara to Savannah to get "real" ice to make ice cream; we can make ice cream every day with our present refrigerators.*

| | |
|---|---|
| ½ cup butter or margarine | 1 cup chopped walnut meats |
| 1 cup sugar | 1 teaspoon vanilla extract |
| 3 egg yolks | Few grains salt |
| 1 cup chopped raisins | 1 egg white |

Pastry (see page 42)

Cream the butter or margarine; add sugar gradually, continuing to cream until smooth. Beat egg yolks; stir into creamed butter. Stir in raisins, walnut meats, vanilla extract and salt. Beat egg white stiff but not dry; fold into the mixture. Line individual tart pans with pastry; fill ⅔ full with filling mixture. Bake in hot oven (400 degrees F.) for 10 minutes. Reduce heat to moderate (350 degrees F.), bake 15 minutes longer. Makes 8 to 9 tarts.

### ➤➤ SYLLABUB ➤

2 cups heavy cream         ⅛ cup confectioners' sugar
4 tablespoons sherry flavoring

Combine cream with sugar and whip until thick; slowly stir in sherry. Serve at once with lady fingers. Makes 6 servings.

### ➤➤ TWELVE OAKS PLUM PUDDING ➤

| | |
|---|---|
| 1¾ cups flour | ½ cup lukewarm water |
| 1 teaspoon baking soda | 1 egg, beaten |
| ½ teaspoon salt | ½ cup seeded raisins |
| 1 teaspoon cinnamon | ½ cup chopped dates |
| ½ teaspoon nutmeg | ½ cup currants |
| ½ cup molasses | |

2 tablespoons melted butter or margarine

Mix and sift flour, soda, salt and spices into mixing bowl. Mix molasses and water, stir into dry ingredients. Add beaten egg; combine thoroughly. Stir in fruits and butter or margarine. Fill greased pudding mold ¾ full; cover tightly. Steam 2 hours. Serve hot with Hard Sauce. Makes 8 servings.

### ➤➤ PLUM PUDDING ➤

| | |
|---|---|
| ½ pound beef suet | 1 cup milk |
| 1 cup sugar | ¼ teaspoon salt |
| 4 eggs, well beaten | Grated rind 1 small lemon |
| 1 cup flour | ½ pound raisins |
| 1 teaspoon cinnamon | ¼ pound currants |
| ½ teaspoon mace | ½ pound almonds, shredded |
| 1 cup bread crumbs | ½ nutmeg, grated |

½ cup sherry flavoring

Chop suet fine and mix well with sugar. Add the beaten eggs. Mix half the flour with the spices, and use remaining half to dredge the fruit and nuts. Add the flour and spices and the bread crumbs to suet mixture; then stir in sherry, milk, salt and grated lemon rind. Add the fruit and nuts, blend thoroughly and turn into a greased mold. Steam 2 to 2½ hours. Serve with Hard Sauce. Makes about 10 servings.

### ➤➤ HARD SAUCE ➤

½ cup butter or margarine       2 cups confectioners' sugar
2 tablespoons brandy or sherry

Cream butter or margarine; add sugar gradually; cream thoroughy. Add brandy or sherry. Beat until light. Serves 8.

## ➤➤ AUNT PITTYPAT'S COCONUT PUDDING ➤

| | |
|---|---|
| 2 teaspoons cornstarch | ½ teaspoon vanilla extract |
| ¾ cup sugar | ⅛ teaspoon almond extract |
| ¼ teaspoon salt | ½ cup toasted coconut |
| 2 cups milk | 3 egg whites |
| 3 egg yolks | |

Combine cornstarch, 4 tablespoons sugar and salt; stir in milk gradually. Cook over hot water until slightly thickened, stirring constantly. Beat egg yolks; stir in hot milk mixture slowly. Cook over hot water until mixture coats spoon, stirring constantly. Cool. Add vanilla and almond extracts. Pour into shallow baking dish; sprinkle with coconut. Beat egg whites until stiff but not dry; add remaining ½ cup sugar gradually, beating constantly. Drop by spoonfuls on custard. Bake in moderately slow oven (325 degrees F.) for 15 minutes, until brown. Cool. Makes 4 to 6 servings.

## ➤➤ DIXIE CHOCOLATE SOUFFLÉ ➤

| | |
|---|---|
| 2 tablespoons butter or margarine | 3 squares (3 ounces) unsweetened |
| 3 tablespoons flour | chocolate |
| Few grains salt | 3 tablespoons hot water |
| 1 cup milk | 1 teaspoon vanilla extract |
| ½ cup sugar | 3 egg yolks |
| 3 egg whites | ½ cup heavy cream |

Melt butter or margarine; add flour and salt. Mix well. Stir in milk gradually; cook over hot water until thick, stirring constantly. Stir in sugar. Cut chocolate in small pieces; add water; melt over hot water. Add to first mixture with vanilla extract; mix well. Beat egg yolks; stir into chocolate mixture. Beat egg whites stiff but not dry; fold in. Pour into greased baking dish; bake in moderately slow oven (325 degrees F.) for 50 to 60 minutes. Serve immediately. Whip cream; serve on soufflé. Makes 4 to 6 servings.

## ➤➤ STRAWBERRY WHIP ➤

| | |
|---|---|
| 3 egg whites | 3 tablespoons sugar |
| Few grains salt | 1 tablespoon lemon juice |
| 1½ cups crushed sweetened strawberries | |

Beat egg whites stiff but not dry; add salt and sugar gradually, beating constantly. Add lemon juice to strawberries; fold into egg whites. Beat until fluffy; pile in sherbet glasses. Chill. Serve plain or with a custard sauce. Makes 6 servings.

## ━► LEMON SOUFFLE ◄━

4 egg yolks
1 cup sugar
Juice of 1 lemon

Grated rind of 1 lemon
Few grains salt
4 egg whites

Beat egg yolks until thick and lemon colored. Add ½ cup sugar gradually, beating constantly. Add lemon juice, rind and salt. Beat egg whites stiff but not dry; carefully fold in remaining ½ cup sugar. Fold in egg yolk mixture. Pour into greased baking dish. Bake in moderately slow oven (325 degrees F.) for 50 to 60 minutes. Serve immediately. Makes 4 servings.

## ━► KENTUCKY STRAWBERRY SHORTCAKE ◄━

1 quart strawberries
1 cup sugar
2 cups flour
½ teaspoon salt

1 teaspoon baking powder
⅔ cup shortening
Ice water (about 6 tablespoons)
1 cup heavy cream

Wash berries; hull. Reserve few for garnish; crush remaining berries. Add sugar; chill. Mix and sift flour, salt and baking powder. Cut in shortening with 2 knives or pastry blender. Add enough ice water to hold ingredients together. Divide pastry into 3 equal parts. Roll out each part on slightly floured board; cut in 8-inch circle. Bake in 3 separate layer cake pans in hot oven (425 degrees F.) 15 minutes or until golden brown. Put crushed strawberries between circles of pastry; garnish top with whole strawberries. Serve immediately with plain or whipped cream. Makes 6 servings. (For shortcakes made with Biscuit dough, see page 22.)

## ━► GEORGIA PEACH TRIFLE ◄━

2 teaspoons cornstarch
½ cup sugar
Few grains salt
2 cups milk

3 egg yolks
½ teaspoon vanilla extract
Stale sponge cake
2 cups sliced fresh peaches

Combine cornstarch, ¼ cup sugar and salt. Stir in milk gradually. Cook over hot water until slightly thickened, stirring constantly. Beat egg yolks; stir in hot milk mixture slowly. Cook over hot water until mixture coats spoon, stirring constantly. Cool. Add vanilla extract. Slice sponge cake thin. Add remaining ¼ cup sugar to peaches. Arrange cake and peaches in alternate layers. Top with custard sauce. Chill. Makes 4 to 6 servings.

# MELANIE'S SWEET POTATO PIE

2 cups mashed, cooked sweet potatoes
½ cup brown sugar, firmly packed
¼ teaspoon salt
1 teaspoon cinnamon
⅛ teaspoon nutmeg
4 egg yolks
⅛ cup melted butter or margarine
2 cups milk
4 egg whites
9-inch unbaked pie shell (see page 42)

Combine sweet potatoes, sugar, salt, cinnamon and nutmeg. Beat egg yolks; add with butter or margarine to potato mixture. Mix well. Add milk and combine. Beat egg whites stiff but not dry; fold into the mixture. Pour into unbaked pie shell. Bake in hot oven (425 degrees F.) for 15 minutes. Reduce heat to moderately hot (375 degrees F.), and bake 25 minutes longer, or until firm. Cool. Makes 6 servings.

# ORANGE JELLY

1 envelope (1 tablespoon) unflavored gelatine
¼ cup cold water
⅓ cup sugar
Few grains salt
1 cup hot water
½ cup orange juice
1 tablespoon lemon juice
Orange wedges

Soften gelatine in cold water. Add sugar, salt and hot water; stir until dissolved. Mix in orange and lemon juice. Pour into individual molds which have been rinsed in cold water. Chill until firm. Unmold; garnish with orange wedges. Makes 4 to 6 servings.

# CHARLOTTE RUSSE

2 egg yolks
2 tablespoons sugar
¼ teaspoon salt
1½ cups scalded milk
1 envelope (1 tablespoon) unflavored gelatine
¼ cup cold water
4 egg whites
1 cup heavy cream
1 teaspoon vanilla extract
Lady fingers
Currant jelly

Beat egg yolks; add 2 tablespoons of the sugar gradually, beating constantly. Add salt and milk. Cook over hot water until mixture coats spoon, stirring constantly. Soften gelatine in cold water; add to hot custard; stir until dissolved. Cool slightly. Beat egg whites stiff; fold in. Whip cream; add remaining 3 tablespoons sugar and vanilla extract. Fold in. Line sherbet glasses with lady fingers. Fill with custard mixture. Chill until firm. Garnish each with cube of currant jelly. Makes 6 servings.

[ 41 ]

## ⚜ FLAKY PASTRY ⚜

2 cups sifted all-purpose flour  
½ teaspoon salt  

⅔ cup shortening  
Cold water (about 6 tablespoons)

Mix and sift flour and salt. Cut shortening into flour with 2 knives or pasty blender. Add enough water to hold ingredients together, sprinkling it in evenly and mixing with a fork. Wrap dough in waxed paper; chill ½ to 1 hour before rolling. Divide dough in half. Roll on lightly-floured board to ⅛-inch thickness for pies and pie shells. Bake pie shells in very hot oven (450 degrees F.) for 15 minutes. Makes enough pastry for 1 double-crust (9-inch) pie or 2 (9-inch) pie shells.

## ⚜ CARAMEL NUT PIE ⚜

1 cup brown sugar  
¼ teaspoon salt  
3 tablespoons flour  
2 eggs  
1 cup milk  

3 tablespoons butter or margarine  
1 teaspoon vanilla extract  
½ cup broken walnut meats  
8-inch baked pie shell (see page 42)  
1 cup heavy cream

Mix sugar, salt and flour. Beat eggs; add milk, and stir into sugar mixture. Cook over hot water until thick, stirring constantly. Cover; cook 10 minutes longer. Remove from heat; stir in butter or margarine, vanilla extract and walnut meats. Pour into baked pie shell; cool. Whip cream, flavor and sweeten. Swirl on pie. Makes 6 servings.

## ⚜ EGG NOG ICE CREAM ⚜

2 cups milk  
1 cup sugar  
1 tablespoon flour  

Dash salt  
4 egg yolks, slightly beaten  
2 teaspoons rum flavoring  

2 cups light cream

Scald milk in double boiler. Mix sugar, flour and salt. Add to milk, and cook 5 minutes, stirring constantly. Stir a small amount into egg yolks, return to double boiler and cook 2 minutes, stirring constantly. Chill; add rum flavoring, and cream. Pour into container of freezer. It should not be more than ⅔ full; adjust dasher and cover tightly. Place in tub of freezer. Pour a 2-inch layer of finely cracked ice in tub, add a layer of salt and continue to fill with ice and salt until tub is ¾ full. Use the proportions 8-10 parts ice to 1 part rock salt. At first turn handle slowly until mixture seems somewhat thickened. Then turn rapidly until frozen—about 15 minutes in all. Drain off excess brine. Wipe off top and remove cover, take out dasher; press down frozen mixture. Replace cover and close opening in lid with a cork. Replace in ice and salt, covering the container completely, using the proportions 3 or 4 parts ice to 1 part salt. Cover freezer with a heavy canvas or paper and let ripen 3 to 4 hours. Makes about 3 pints or 8 to 10 servings.

## BAKED ALASKA

| | |
|---|---|
| Sponge cake | 5 egg whites |
| 1 quart mold of ice cream | ¾ cup sugar |

Cut sponge cake 1 inch thick and about ½ inch wider and longer than quart mold of ice cream. Place cake in baking sheet. Beat egg whites stiff but not dry; add sugar gradually, beating constantly. Put mold of ice cream on cake; cover top and sides with meringue. Bake in very hot oven (500 degrees F.) for 2 or 3 minutes to brown meringue. Serve at once. Makes 6 to 8 servings.

## PLANTATION PUMPKIN PIE

| | |
|---|---|
| 2 cups strained cooked pumpkin | ¼ teaspoon nutmeg |
| ½ cup sugar | 1 teaspoon salt |
| 1½ teaspoons cinnamon | 3 egg yolks |
| ¼ teaspoon cloves | 1 cup milk |
| ½ teaspoon ginger | 3 egg whites |
| 9-inch unbaked pie shell (see page 42) | |

Combine pumpkin, sugar, cinnamon, cloves, ginger, nutmeg and salt. Beat egg yolks; stir into first mixture. Add milk. Beat egg whites stiff; fold into the mixture. Pour into unbaked pie shell. Bake in very hot oven (450 degrees F.) for 10 minutes. Reduce heat to moderately hot (375 degrees F.) and bake 20 minutes longer, or until filling is firm. Makes 6 servings.

## COCONUT CREAM PIE

| | |
|---|---|
| ⅔ cup sugar | 2 cups milk |
| 8½ tablespoons flour | 1 teaspoon vanilla extract |
| Few grains salt | 9-inch baked pie shell (see page 42) |
| 3 egg yolks | 1 cup heavy cream |
| Fresh grated coconut | |

Mix sugar, flour and salt. Beat egg yolks; add milk, and stir into sugar mixture. Cook over hot water until thick, stirring constantly. Cover; cook 10 minutes longer. Cool slightly; add vanilla extract. Pour into baked pie shell; cool. Just before serving, whip cream until stiff. Flavor and sweeten if desired. Spread on pie. Sprinkle generously with coconut. Makes 6 servings.

## ►►◄ SOUTHERN PECAN PIE ►◄◄

¼ cup butter or margarine
⅔ cup firmly packed brown sugar
Dash of salt
¾ cup dark corn syrup

3 eggs, well beaten
1 cup pecan halves
1 teaspoon vanilla extract
8-inch unbaked pie shell (see page 42)

Cream together butter or margarine, brown sugar and salt; stir in remaining ingredients. Pour into unbaked pie shell. Bake in very hot oven (450 degrees F.) for 10 minutes; then reduce heat to moderate (350 degrees F.) and bake 30 to 35 minutes longer, or until knife inserted comes out clean. Cool and serve with whipped cream, if desired. Makes 6 servings.

## ►►◄ APPLE SCALLOP ►◄◄

1 cup flour
¼ cup brown sugar, firmly packed
½ cup butter or margarine

¼ cup finely chopped nut meats
4 cups sliced apples
Cinnamon and nutmeg

Cream

Mix flour and sugar; cut in butter or margarine with 2 knives or pastry blender. Add nut meats. Place apples in greased baking dish; sprinkle with cinnamon and nutmeg; cover with flour mixture. Bake in moderately hot oven (375 degrees F.) for 45 minutes, or until apples are tender. Serve with cream. Makes 6 servings.

## ►►◄ AMBROSIA ►◄◄

6 oranges
⅓ cup sugar
1 tablespoon sherry flavoring

1⅓ cups of fresh coconut
(OR 4-ounce can moist pack coconut)

Peel oranges, removing all outside membrane. Cut in thin slices. Place alternate layers of oranges, coconut and sugar in serving dish. Sprinkle with sherry flavoring. Press down with plate; chill ½ hour. Makes 6 servings.

## ►►◄ FROZEN SYLLABUB ►◄◄

½ cup milk
½ cup sweet cider
½ teaspoon vanilla extract

½ cup sugar
1 tablespoon sherry flavoring
1 cup heavy cream

Combine milk, cider, vanilla extract, sugar and sherry flavoring. Mix well. Whip cream until slightly thickened; combine with milk mixture. Pour into tray of automatic refrigerator and freeze at point recommended for freezing ice cream. Do not stir. Makes 4 to 6 servings.

# ⊂ BEVERAGES ⊃

## ➤ EGGNOG ➤

| | |
|---|---|
| 1 cup granulated sugar | 1 pint whipping cream |
| 12 eggs | Nutmeg to taste |
| 1 pint Bourbon, rye, cognac brandy | |
| or Jamaica rum | |

Separate the eggs. Beat egg yolks, adding sugar gradually, until thick and lemon colored. Then add the Bourbon, rye, brandy or rum slowly, stirring constantly. Fold in the whipped cream, and then the beaten egg whites. Add grated nutmeg when serving. Makes 12 servings.

## ➤ EGGNOG BEVERAGE ➤

| | |
|---|---|
| 10 eggs | 1 pint milk |
| ½ cup granulated sugar | 1 pint heavy cream |
| 1 pint Bourbon, rye, cognac brandy | 1 pint vanilla ice cream |
| or Jamaica rum | Nutmeg to taste |

Separate the eggs. Beat yolks, adding sugar gradually, until thick and lemon colored. Then beat in the Bourbon, rye, brandy or rum slowly, stirring constantly. Add milk and cream gradually. Fold in stiffly beaten egg whites, and mix thoroughly. Serve with a small spoonful of ice cream and top with a little grated nutmeg. Makes 16 servings.

## ➤ CLARET PUNCH ➤

| | |
|---|---|
| 2 quarts claret | ½ cup brandy |
| 2 pints soda water | 1 cup granulated sugar |
| 1 pint sherry | 2 lemons, sliced |
| Crushed ice | |

Mix claret, soda water, sherry and brandy with sugar. Chill and pour in punch glasses over crushed ice. Serve with a thin slice of lemon. This makes 4 quarts of punch or fills 30 punch glasses.

# SWEETS

## ➤ PEANUT BRITTLE ➤

1½ cups shelled roasted peanuts    ½ cup light corn syrup
¼ teaspoon salt                    ½ cup water
1 cup granulated sugar             1½ tablespoons butter or margarine
                  ½ teaspoon vanilla extract

Chop peanuts, then sprinkle with salt, and warm in the oven. Mix sugar, syrup and water together; heat slowly, stirring until sugar is dissolved. Cook over moderate heat until thermometer registers 265 degrees F., or a small amount of mixture forms a hard ball when dropped in cold water. Then add butter or margarine, and cook slowly to 290 degrees F., or until brittle threads form when a small amount is dropped in cold water. Remove from heat; stir in warm nuts and vanilla extract. Pour immediately on greased baking pan in thin sheet.

*Brazil Nut Brittle:* Use Brazil nuts in above recipe. Shave nuts in thin slices; toast in moderate oven (350 degrees F.) before adding.

## ➤ PECAN PRALINES ➤

1 cup brown sugar         1 tablespoon butter or margarine
1 cup granulated sugar    ⅛ teaspoon salt
1 cup milk                1 cup chopped pecans
                1 tablespoon maple syrup

Combine sugars and milk; cook over low heat, stirring constantly until sugars are dissolved and mixture boils. Continue cooking, stirring frequently, over a moderate heat until thermometer registers 224 degrees F. Add butter or margarine, salt, and pecans, and cook to 234 degrees F., or until a small amount of mixture forms a soft ball when dropped in cold water. Cool quickly to lukewarm (110 degrees F.) Stir in the maple syrup and heat until thick. Drop on a buttered surface and flatten out into patties. Makes 1 dozen.

# INDEX

# MY FAVORITE "GONE WITH THE WIND" DINNER PARTY MENUS

# MY BEST "GONE WITH THE WIND" LUNCHEON PARTY MENUS

# DELICIOUS SOUTHERN
# SUNDAY NIGHT SUPPER MENUS

# OTHER SCRUMPTIOUS SOUTHERN RECIPES

# MY OWN SOUTHERN DESSERTS

# METRIC CONVERSIONS

## Weights and Measures

| Deg. C | °F or °C | Deg. F | Deg. C | °F or °C | Deg. F | Deg. C | °F or °C | Deg. F |
|--------|----------|--------|--------|----------|--------|--------|----------|--------|
| 74.4 | 166 | 330.8 | 83.3 | 182 | 359.6 | 92.2 | 198 | 388.4 |
| 75.0 | 167 | 332.6 | 83.9 | 183 | 361.4 | 92.8 | 199 | 390.2 |
| 75.6 | 168 | 334.4 | 84.4 | 184 | 363.2 | 93.3 | 200 | 392.0 |
| 76.1 | 169 | 336.2 | 85.0 | 185 | 365.0 | 93.9 | 201 | 393.8 |
| 76.7 | 170 | 338.0 | 85.6 | 186 | 366.8 | 94.4 | 202 | 395.6 |
| 77.2 | 171 | 339.8 | 86.1 | 187 | 368.6 | 95.0 | 203 | 397.4 |
| 77.8 | 172 | 341.6 | 86.7 | 188 | 370.4 | 95.6 | 204 | 399.2 |
| 78.3 | 173 | 343.4 | 87.2 | 189 | 372.2 | 96.1 | 205 | 401.0 |
| 78.9 | 174 | 345.2 | 87.8 | 190 | 374.0 | 96.7 | 206 | 402.8 |
| 79.4 | 175 | 347.0 | 88.3 | 191 | 375.8 | 97.2 | 207 | 404.6 |
| 80.0 | 176 | 348.8 | 88.9 | 192 | 377.6 | 97.8 | 208 | 406.4 |
| 80.5 | 177 | 350.6 | 89.4 | 193 | 379.4 | 98.3 | 209 | 408.2 |
| 81.1 | 178 | 352.4 | 90.0 | 194 | 381.2 | 98.9 | 210 | 410.0 |
| 81.7 | 179 | 354.2 | 90.6 | 195 | 383.0 | 99.4 | 211 | 411.8 |
| 82.2 | 180 | 356.0 | 91.1 | 196 | 384.8 | 100.0 | 212 | 413.6 |
| 82.8 | 181 | 357.8 | 91.7 | 197 | 386.6 | | | |

## Converting Household Measurements

| From | To | Multiply by |
|------|-----|-------------|
| units | dozens | 12 |
| baker's dozens | units | 13 |
| teaspoons | milliliters | 4.93 |
| teaspoons | tablespoons | 0.33 |
| tablespoons | milliliters | 14.79 |
| tablespoons | teaspoons | 3 |
| cups | liters | 0.24 |
| cups | pints | 0.50 |
| cups | quarts | 0.25 |
| pints | cups | 2 |
| pints | liters | 0.47 |
| pints | quarts | 0.50 |
| quarts | cups | 4 |
| quarts | gallons | 0.25 |
| quarts | liters | 0.95 |
| quarts | pints | 2 |
| gallons | liters | 3.79 |
| gallons | quarts | 4 |

## Metric Conversion

1 teaspoon = 4.93 milliliters

1/2 teaspoon = 2.47 milliliters

1/4 teaspoon = 1.23 milliliters

1 tablespoon = 14.79 milliliters

1/2 tablespoon = 7.4 milliliters

1 cup = .24 liters

1/2 cup = .12 liters

1 pint = .47 liters

1 quart = .95 liters

1 gallon = 3.79 liters